SRA Imagine It!

Red, White, and Blue

Level K
Unit 9

McGraw Hill SRA

COLUMBUS, OH

Program Authors

Carl Bereiter	Steve Graham	Michael Pressley
Andy Biemiller	Karen Harris	Marsha Roit
Joe Campione	Jan Hirshberg	Marlene Scardamalia
Iva Carruthers	Anne McKeough	Marcy Stein
Doug Fuchs	Peter Pannell	Gerald H. Treadway Jr.
Lynn Fuchs		

Acknowledgments

Grateful acknowledgment is given to the following publishers and copyright owners for permissions granted to reprint selections from their publications. All possible care has been taken to trace ownership and secure permission for each selection included. In case of any errors or omissions, the Publisher will be pleased to make suitable acknowledgments in future editions.

F IS FOR FLAG by Wendy Cheyette Lewison. Text copyright © by Wendy Cheyette Lewison, 2002. Illustrations copyright © by Barbara Duke, 2002. Published by arrangement with Grosset and Dunlap, a division of Penguin Young Readers Group, a division of Penguin Group (USA) Inc. All rights reserved.

"Celebrate" from COME TO MY PARTY AND OTHER SHAPE POEMS by Heidi B. Roemer, illustrated by Hideko Takahashi. Reprinted by permission of Henry Holt and Company, LLC.

From HATS OFF FOR THE FOURTH OF JULY by Harriet Ziefert and illustrated by Gustaf Miller. Text Copyright © Harriet Ziefert, 2000. Illustrations Copyright © Gustaf Miller, 2000. All rights reserved including the right of reproduction in whole or in part in any form. This edition is published by arrangement with Viking Children's Books, a member of Penguin Young Readers Group, a division of Penguin Group (USA) Inc.

Reprinted with permission of Atheneum Books for Young Readers, an imprint of Simon & Schuster Children's Publishing Division from AMERICA THE BEAUTIFUL by Katharine Lee Bates, illustrated by Neil Waldman. Illustrations copyright © 1993 Neil Waldman.

Photo Credits

TOC (cr) © Carlos Pascual/Overseas Arts, LLC; 54 (tr) © Daniel Chester French, (cl) © William H. Johnson/Smithsonian American Art Museum, Washington, D.C., (br) © Carlos Pascual/Overseas Arts, LLC.

SRAonline.com

SRA

Send all inquiries to:
SRA/McGraw-Hill
4400 Easton Commons
Columbus, OH 43219

ISBN: 978-0-07-609632-9
MHID: 0-07-609632-7

1 2 3 4 5 6 7 8 9 RRM 15 14 13 12 11 10 09 08 07

The McGraw-Hill Companies

Red, White, and Blue
Table of Contents

F IS FOR FLAG

by Wendy Cheyette Lewison

illustrated by Barbara Duke

F is for "flag." Our flag.

The American flag.

See it waving in the wind,
just like a hand waving hello.

Our flag is everywhere—at the library and in the park, even on letters we send. We see our flag near and far. At school . . .

. . . and on ships at sea.

We see our flag—in happy times and sad times.

Our flag is so many places because we are proud of it.

It stands for our country, the United States of America.

And it stands for us, the people who live here.

Who are we?

We are all kinds of people—
different in many ways.

But we live and work and play together.

We are like one great big family.

One country, one family, one flag for everybody.

The first American flag was made more than 200 years ago. That's when America became a country. Who made the first flag? No one really knows. One story says Betsy Ross made it after George Washington asked her to.

Snip, snip, snip! Betsy cut and sewed.
Soon the flag was finished.

The first flag looked different. It had 13 stars and 13 stripes. That's because there were only 13 states when the United States first became a country. Today our country is bigger.

We have 50 states now, and our flag has
50 bright stars, one for each state. But our
flag still has 13 stripes to remember the first
13 states.

The colors of our flag are the same—red, white, and blue. Sometimes we even call our flag the "Red, White, and Blue." We've given our flag a nickname.

We have other nicknames for our flag, too—"Stars and Stripes," "Old Glory," and "Star-Spangled Banner."

19

"The Star-Spangled Banner" is also
the name of our country's song.

It's a song all about our flag. Sometimes when we hear it, tears come to our eyes.

We are proud of our flag. We have songs about it.

We have nicknames for it. We have the Pledge of Allegiance, too.

The Pledge of Allegiance

I pledge Allegiance to the flag of the United States of America and to the republic for which it stands one nation under God indivisible with liberty and justice for all.

The Pledge is a promise—a promise to be a good American, a promise to be a good friend to our flag. As we make this promise, we hold our hand over our heart. This shows that we mean what we say.

WELCOME TO OUR CLASS

GOOD MORNING CLASS

F is for "flag." Our flag.

F is for family and friends and freedom, too—and everything special that our flag stands for.

F is also for Flag Day—June 14—our flag's birthday.

On Flag Day, big parades march down streets all over America.

Boom, boom, boom! go the drums.

Here comes the Red, White, and Blue!

Hooray for our flag—today . . .

. . . and every day!

Focus Question How are the people celebrating?

Celebrate

by Heidi B. Roemer

illustrated by Hideko Takahashi

It's a day for parades and for clowns who say "hi!"

For loud marching bands and balloons in the sky.

It's a flag-waving day! Here's a flag just for you.

Hooray for parades and the red, white, and blue!

We love parades.

Hats Off for the Fourth of July!

by Harriet Ziefert

illustrated by Gustaf Miller

In Chatham town on the Fourth of July,
A grand parade will go marching by.

Music and drum . . . music and drum.

We're all waiting to see it come.

The twirlers are walking down the street.

They spin and strut and lift their feet.

Music and drum . . . music and drum.

Who will be the next to come?

Cowboys on horses yell out loud.

We all shout back—what a happy crowd.

Music and drum . . . music and drum.

Who will be the next to come?

The big kids sit on top of the whale.

I'll ride next year right near his tail.

Music and drum . . . music and drum.

Miss Eelgrass will be the next to come.

She's the favorite of Chatham town.

Her hair is green and wraps around.

Music and boom . . . music and boom!
The big bass drum should be coming soon.

The high school band proudly marches by.

What a sunny day! What a bright blue sky!

Music and vroom. Music and vroom!

The motorcycles need plenty of room.

Patriots march with their muskets and hats.

The Little League follows with baseball bats.

Everyone marches on the Fourth of July.

Hats off! The flag is passing by!

Music and drum . . . music and drum.

We're sorry that the end has come.

The parade is over, but look in the sky.

Hooray for us all on the Fourth of July!

America the Beautiful

by Katharine Lee Bates

illustrated by Neil Waldman

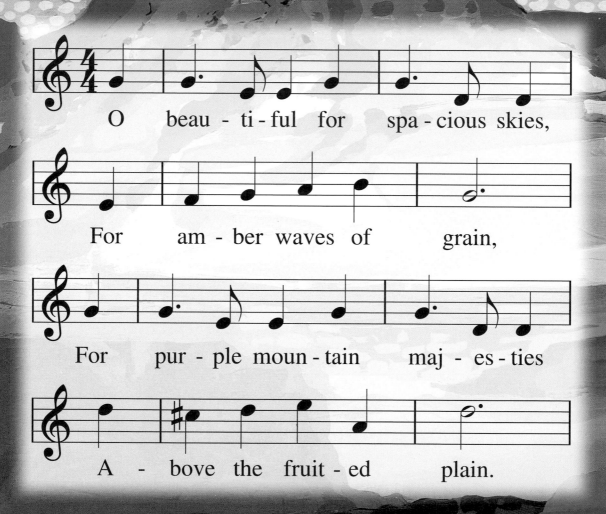

O beau - ti - ful for spa - cious skies,

For am - ber waves of grain,

For pur - ple moun - tain maj - es - ties

A - bove the fruit - ed plain.

Red, White, and Blue

Daniel Chester French.
Lincoln Memorial Statue.
2005.

Georgia Marble. 19 ft.
Washington, D.C.

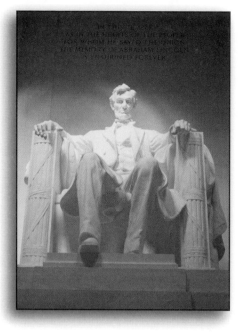

William Johnson. *Lift Up Thy Voice*
2.

d. 64.9 × 54 cm. Smithsonian
useum, Washington, D.C.

Carlos Pascual. *Bald Eagle.*
Argentina. 2006.

Colored pencil. 14″ (H) × 11″ (W).
Private Collection. Wilmington, Delaware.

Glossary

C

clowns

The **clowns** give balloons to the children.

G

grain

The farmer grows **grain** in his field.

M

marching bands

The **marching bands**
play music at the game.

P

parades

We watch many **parades**
in the summer.

plain

Horses run on the **plain**.

S

states

There are fifty **states** in the United States.

strut

The drum majors **strut** in the parade.

T

twirlers

The **twirlers** wear bright costumes.

W

waving

Our flag is **waving** in the wind.

wraps

The snake **wraps** around the tree branch.